SHEMOT / EXODUS

Activity Book

Torah Portion Activity Book: Shemot/Exodus

All rights reserved. By purchasing this Activity Book, the buyer is permitted to copy the activity sheets for personal and classroom use only, but not for commercial resale. With the exception of the above, this Activity Book may not be reproduced in whole or in part in any manner without written permission of the publisher.

Bible Pathway Adventures® is a trademark of BPA Publishing Ltd.
Defenders of the Faith® is a trademark of BPA Publishing Ltd.

ISBN: 978-1-98-858535-2

Author: Pip Reid

Creative Director: Curtis Reid

For free Bible resources including coloring pages, worksheets, puzzles and more, visit our website at:

www.biblepathwayadventures.com

◈◇ INTRODUCTION ◇◈

Your students will LOVE learning about the Torah with our *Shemot / Exodus Torah Portion Activity Book*. We've packed each Torah portion with Bible quizzes, worksheets, puzzles, and questions to help educators just like you teach children the Biblical faith in a fun and engaging way. The perfect resource for your Sabbath or Sunday School class, and homeschooling. Includes scripture references for easy Bible verse look-up, and a handy answer key for educators.

Bible Pathway Adventures helps parents and educators teach children the Biblical faith through illustrated storybooks, Activity Books, and printable resources – all available on our website www.biblepathwayadventures.com

Thanks for buying this Activity Book and supporting our ministry. Every book purchased helps us continue our work providing free Classroom Packs and discipleship materials to families and missions around the world.

__The search for Truth is more fun than Tradition!__

◆◇ TABLE OF CONTENTS ◇◆

Introduction 3

Weekly Torah study guide 8
The Hebrew Alphabet 9

Shemot
Shemot Torah quiz 12
Shemot Prophets quiz 13
Shemot Apostles quiz 14
Shemot word search 15
Shemot worksheet 16
Worksheet: The Israelites are slaves 17
Let's learn Hebrew: Shemot 18
Shemot: Let's discuss… 19

Va'eira
Va'eira Torah quiz 20
Va'eira Prophets quiz 21
Va'eira Apostles quiz 22
Va'eira word search 23
Va'eira worksheet 24
Worksheet: Plague of frogs 25
Let's learn Hebrew: Va'eira 26
Va'eira: Let's discuss… 27

Bo
Bo Torah quiz 28
Bo Prophets quiz 29
Bo Apostles quiz 30
Bo word search 31
Bo worksheet 32
Coloring page: The Passover 33
Let's learn Hebrew: Bo 34
Bo: Let's discuss… 35

Beshalach
Beshalach Torah quiz 36
Beshalach Prophets quiz 37
Beshalach Apostles quiz 38
Beshalach word search 39
Beshalach worksheet 40
Coloring page: Food in the wilderness 41
Let's learn Hebrew: Beshalach 42
Beshalach: Let's discuss… 43

Yitro
Yitro Torah quiz 44
Yitro Prophets quiz 45
Yitro Apostles quiz 46
Yitro word search 47
Yitro worksheet 48
Worksheet: The ten commandments 49
Let's learn Hebrew: Yitro 50
Yitro: Let's discuss… 51

Mishpatim
Mishpatim Torah quiz 52
Mishpatim Prophets quiz 53
Mishpatim Apostles quiz 54
Mishpatim word search 55
Mishpatim worksheet 56
Worksheet: The Promised Land 57
Let's learn Hebrew: Mishpatim 58
Mishpatim: Let's discuss… 59

Terumah

Terumah Torah quiz 60
Terumah Prophets quiz 61
Terumah Apostles quiz 62
Terumah word search 63
Terumah worksheet 64
Worksheet: Ark of the Covenant 65
Let's learn Hebrew: Terumah 66
Terumah: Let's discuss… 67

Tetzaveh

Tetzaveh Torah quiz 68
Tetzaveh Prophets quiz 69
Tetzaveh Apostles quiz 70
Tetzaveh word search 71
Tetzaveh worksheet 72
Worksheet: The high priest 73
Let's learn Hebrew: Tetzaveh 74
Tetzaveh: Let's discuss… 75

Ki Tisa

Ki Tisa Torah quiz 76
Ki Tisa Prophets quiz 77
Ki Tisa Apostles quiz 78
Ki Tisa word search 79
Ki Tisa worksheet 80
Coloring page: The golden calf 81
Let's learn Hebrew: Ki Tisa 82
Ki Tisa: Let's discuss… 83

Vayakhel

Vayakhel Torah quiz 84
Vayakhel Prophets quiz 85
Vayakhel Apostles quiz 86
Vayakhel word search 87
Vayakhel worksheet 88
Worksheet: The Tabernacle 89
Let's learn Hebrew: Vayakhel 90
Vayakhel: Let's discuss… 91

Pekudei

Pekudei Torah quiz 92
Pekudei Prophets quiz 93
Pekudei Apostles quiz 94
Pekudei word search 95
Pekudei worksheet 96
Coloring page: The Levites 97
Let's learn Hebrew: Pekudei 98
Pekudei: Let's discuss… 99

Answer Key 100
Discover more Activity Books! 107

Weekly Torah study guide

With readings from the Prophets and the Apostles

Parashah	Torah Reading	Prophets Reading	Apostles Reading
Shemot	Exodus 1:1-6:1	Isaiah 27:6–28:13; 29:22-23	Hebrews 11:23-27 Acts 7:17-35 Luke 20:37
Va'eira	Exodus 6:2-9:35	Ezekiel 28:25–29:21	Romans 9:14–17 Acts 7:7,17–35 1 Cor 3:11–15
Bo	Exodus 10:1-13:16	Jeremiah 46:13-28	John 19:1-37 Acts 13:16-17 2 Cor 6:14-7:1
Beshalach	Exodus 13:17-17:16	Judges 4:4-5:31	1 Cor 10:1-13 Revelation 15:1-4 Romans 9:15-23
Yitro	Exodus 18:1-20:26	Isaiah 6:1-7:6, 9:6-7	Matthew 19:16-30 1 Timothy 3:1-3 James 2:8-13
Mishpatim	Exodus 21:1-24:18	Jeremiah 34:8-22, 33:25-26	James 3:2-12 Matthew 5:38-42 Hebrews 12:25-29
Terumah	Exodus 25:1-27:19	1 Kings 5:26-5:13	Hebrews 13:10-12 Matthew 5:14-16 Hebrews 10:19-22
Tetzaveh	Exodus 27:20-30:10	Ezekiel 43:10-27	Hebrews 5:1-10 Hebrews 13:10-17 Romans 12:1
Ki Tisa	Exodus 30:11-34:35	1 Kings 18:1-39	1 Cor 12:1-31 Acts 7:39-42 Hebrews 3:1-6
Vayakhel	Exodus 35:1-38:20	1 Kings 7:13-26, 40-50	Hebrews 9:1-28 2 Cor 9:1-15 Hebrews 10:26-31
Pekudei	Exodus 38:21-40:38	1 Kings 7:51-8:21	1 Cor 3:1-17 Hebrews 5:1-11 Hebrews 7:1-8:6

Let's learn Hebrew

The Hebrew alphabet has 22 letters.

Use this chart to guide you as you learn the Hebrew word for each Torah Portion.

Let's write!

Practice writing these Hebrew letters on the lines below.
Remember that Hebrew is written from RIGHT to LEFT.

א
ב
ג
ד
ה
ו

Let's write!

Practice writing these Hebrew letters on the lines below.
Remember that Hebrew is written from RIGHT to LEFT.

ג ח מ ע פ א נ ש ת

Shemot
TORAH QUIZ

Read Exodus 1:1-6:1. Answer the questions below.

1. Why did Pharaoh make the Israelites work as slaves?

2. What instructions did Pharaoh give the Hebrew midwives?

3. Moses was of which tribe of Israel?

4. To which land did Moses flee?

5. Who became Moses' wife?

6. How did the Angel of God (Yeshua) appear to Moses?

7. What instructions did the Angel of God give Moses?

8. What happened when Moses put his hand inside his cloak?

9. With whom did Moses return to Egypt in Exodus 4:29?

10. How did Pharaoh react when Moses asked him to free the Israelites?

Shemot Prophets Quiz

Read Isaiah 27:6-28:13 and 29:22-23. Answer the questions below.

1. "Israel will bud and flower and fill the _____ with a harvest."

2. "He chops up all the _____ stones like chalk…"

3. "Sacred poles and _____ stand no more…"

4. Where will Yah beat out the grain?

5. How will the Israelites be gathered?

6. What will happen on the day the Israelites are gathered?

7. Where will the Israelites come to worship?

8. How will Yah speak to His people?

9. How does the Word of Elohim come to the people?

10. Who did Yah redeem in Isaiah 29:22?

Shemot APOSTLES QUIZ

Read Hebrews 11:23-27, Acts 7:17-35, and Luke 20:37.
Answer the questions below.

1) What did Moses call Yah?

2) For how many months did Moses' parents hide him?

3) What did Moses refuse to be called in Hebrews 11:24?

4) By faith Moses left _____, not being afraid of the king's anger.

5) What was Moses in Yah's eyes?

6) What did Moses learn while growing up in Pharaoh's palace?

7) How old was Moses when he fled the land of Egypt?

8) Where did the Angel of God appear to Moses?

9) What did the angel say to Moses?

10) To which land did Yah send Moses?

Shemot WORD SEARCH

Read Exodus 1:1-6:1. Find and circle the words below.

```
Z P H D D P P W R P X V Z N N
M Z H E Q U J H U W A T I O J
L U C Y B H F N A W S B Y B T
B A D U A R A F B R L I K U R
A H N B I F E H O B A K J R I
S S G D R K G W L K V O M N B
K R N J O I T N S S E K H I E
E C C D P F C Y M O S C F N O
T F H K J S E K X V M Z R G F
P T G X K T I G S H T C X B L
X N C M X R Q K Y I E O A U E
X W B D J A P C U P B K O S V
H Y P U Y W L Y P X T T E H I
N I L E R I V E R M O S E S Q
Y J L A N D O F M I D I A N F
```

SLAVES

LAND OF EGYPT

PHARAOH

BASKET

NILE RIVER

BURNING BUSH

MOSES

MUD BRICKS

HEBREWS

STRAW

LAND OF MIDIAN

TRIBE OF LEVI

All about Shemot...

Draw your favorite scene from this Torah Portion. Use your imagination!

Imagine you are an Israelite slave. Describe how you would make a straw brick.

....
....
....
....
....
....
....
....

This Torah portion teaches me…

....
....
....
....
....
....

Create a map to help Moses find his way to Midian.

The Israelites are slaves

Open your Bibles and read Exodus 1:1-22.
Answer the questions. Color the picture.

1. Why was Pharaoh worried about the Israelites?

   ....
   ....
   ....

2. What did the Egyptians make the Israelites do?

   ....
   ....
   ....

3. What instructions did Pharaoh give the midwives?

   ....
   ....
   ....

Shemot

"Now these are the names of the sons of Israel who came into Egypt;
Reuben, Simeon, Levi, and Judah, Issachar, Zebulun,
and Benjamin, Dan and Naphtali, Gad and Asher."

Exodus 1:1-4

"Names"

Trace the Hebrew word here:

שְׁמוֹת

שְׁמוֹת

Write the Hebrew word here:

Let's discuss...

Open your Bibles and read the Bible verses below.
Discuss these questions with your family, friends, and classmates.

1 **Read Exodus 2:1-4:17 and Acts 7:23.**
Why do you think Moses had to spend 40 years in the wilderness taking care of the sheep? What lessons did Yah need to teach Moses?

2 **Read Exodus 3:1-12 and Galatians 4:25.**
Yah told Moses to return to Mount Sinai to serve Him. Research the location of Mount Sinai. Where was the land of Midian?

3 **Read Exodus 1:1-2:25.**
A metaphor is a word or phrase that means something else. Understanding metaphors helps us understand the Bible. What do you think Egypt, Pharaoh, and Moses are metaphors for?

4 **Read Exodus 6:1.**
Yah promises to deliver the Israelites from slavery in Egypt. Do you believe that Yah always keeps His promises? Where else in scripture can you find examples of where He makes a promise and keeps it? How about your life?

5 **Read Hebrews 11:23-27.**
By faith Moses made some important decisions. How about you? Have you made any decisions that require faith in your Creator?

Va'eira TORAH QUIZ

Read Exodus 6:2-9:35. Answer the questions below.

1. With whom did Yah establish His Covenant?
2. What did Yah promise to do for the Israelites?
3. Who is the firstborn of Israel?
4. What happened when Aaron threw down his staff before Pharaoh?
5. What was the first plague?
6. Which plague could the Egyptian magicians not copy?
7. What was the fourth plague?
8. Whose livestock died in the fifth plague?
9. What was the seventh plague?
10. In which part of the land of Egypt did hailstones not fall?

Va'eira PROPHETS QUIZ

Read Ezekiel 28:25–29:21. Answer the questions below.

1) From where will Yah gather the House of Israel?

2) On whom will Yah execute judgment?

3) About whom was the prophecy given?

4) To what animal does Yah compare Pharaoh?

5) What river runs through the land of Egypt?

6) For how many years will Egypt's cities be laid waste?

7) Where will Yah scatter the Egyptians?

8) What will happen to the Egyptians after forty years?

9) On what date did Ezekiel receive another word from Yah about Egypt?

10) To which king will Yah give the land of Egypt?

Va'eira APOSTLES QUIZ

Read Romans 9:14-17, Acts 7:7, 17-35, and 1 Corinthians 3:11-15.
Answer the questions below.

1. What did Yah say to Moses?

2. Why did Yah raise up Pharaoh?

3. What happened to the Israelites as the time of the promise grew near?

4. Who was beautiful in Yah's sight?

5. Who adopted Moses as her own son?

6. To which land did Moses flee?

7. After how many years did an angel appear to Moses?

8. Why did Yah ask Moses to remove his shoes?

9. To which land did Yah say He was sending Moses?

10. Who is our foundation?

Va'eira WORD SEARCH

Read Exodus 6:2-9:35. Find and circle the words below.

```
K L B A W S S N C J N B C R T
A I A O Y R X Q O T H M Q U E
K V O N I B C P E H H E B J N
U E E Z D L Q F X U Y Y B L P
F S E W E O S V R N G D C A L
C T S W B I F A B D H K L N A
J O G Q S L D G F E F D Q D G
L C Q E H I O N O R U X Y O U
O K V E A K D O M S A B I F E
P B R W B U R F D K H Z J E S
M R I V E R N I L E U E X G Z
M Z G U B A V E X H V V N Y S
P P C A F I E R Y H A I L P R
Q A E U A A R O N Y E P D T N
F L I E S M X M O S E S G F A
```

MOSES

BLOOD

FLIES

LAND OF GOSHEN

BOILS

FIERY HAIL

TEN PLAGUES

LAND OF EGYPT

LIVESTOCK

RIVER NILE

THUNDER

AARON

All about Va'eira...

Draw a picture to show the plague of fiery hail.

Imagine you are an Egyptian magician. What would you say to Pharaoh when you were not able to copy the plague of gnats?

....
....
....
....
....
....
....
....

This Torah portion teaches me…

....
....
....
....
....

Design a staff for Aaron that turns into a serpent. Use your imagination!

Plague of Frogs

Open your Bibles and read Exodus 8:1-15.
Answer the questions. Color the picture.

1. What happened when Aaron stretched out his hand over the waters of Egypt?

   ....
   ....
   ....

2. Who copied this plague?

   ....
   ....
   ....

3. What did Pharaoh do when he saw the frogs had all died?

   ....
   ....
   ....

Va'eira

"Yah spoke to Moses, "I am Yah. I appeared to Abraham, Isaac, and Jacob, as God Almighty; but by my name Yah I was not known to them. I have also established My covenant with them to give them the land of Canaan…"

Exodus 6:2-4

Va'eira

"I appeared"

וָאֵרָא

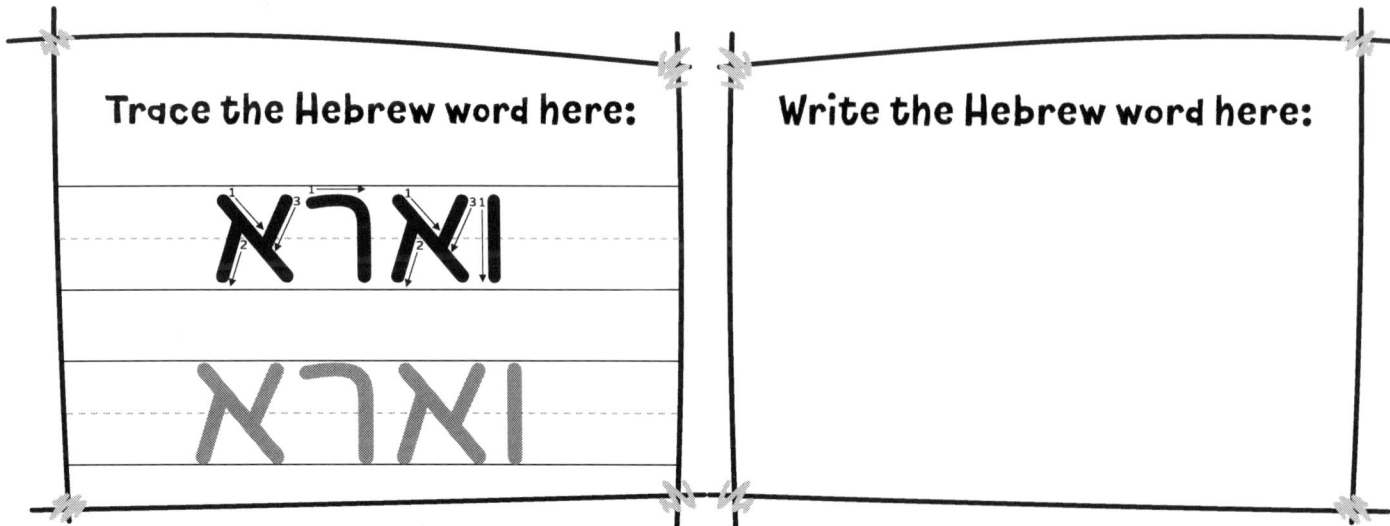

Trace the Hebrew word here:

Write the Hebrew word here:

Let's discuss...

Open your Bibles and read the Bible verses below.
Discuss these questions with your family, friends, and classmates.

1. Read Exodus 6:2-9:35 and Romans 9:17-18.
Yah hardened Pharaoh's heart after each plague. Why do you think Yah did this?

2. Read Exodus 6:9-13.
Why did the Israelites not listen to Moses? How did Yah encourage Moses and Aaron?

3. Read Exodus 6:2-9:35.
What are some similarities between Yeshua and Moses?

4. Read Exodus 6:2-7:13 and Hebrews 11:25.
How would you describe Moses' character?

5. Read Hebrews 11:23-27.
Why did Moses choose to obey Yah instead of staying in Egypt?

6. Read Hebrews 11:23-27.
Did Moses choose to follow the world or Yah? How about you - who has the most influence in your life?

Bo
TORAH QUIZ

Read Exodus 10:1-13:16. Answer the questions below.

1. What type of wind brought the locusts?

2. What did the locusts eat?

3. What was the ninth plague?

4. Why would Pharaoh would not listen to Moses?

5. In which Hebrew month is the Passover?

6. For how long did Yah ask the Israelites to honor the Passover?

7. What type of bread is eaten during the Feast of Unleavened Bread?

8. What was the tenth plague?

9. What did the Egyptians give the Israelites when they left Egypt?

10. How many Israelites left Egypt after the final plague?

Bo
PROPHETS QUIZ

Read Jeremiah 46:13-28. Answer the questions below.

1. Who was Jeremiah?

2. Who was the king of Babylon?

3. Who was the king of Egypt?

4. Who should prepare themselves for exile?

5. Which city will become a wasteland?

6. With what animals are Egypt's hired soldiers compared?

7. With what animal is Egypt compared?

8. Who will defeat the Egyptians?

9. Who will Yah save from the land of their captivity?

10. "Fear not, ____ my servant, declares Yah, for I am with you."

Bo APOSTLES QUIZ

Read John 19:1-37, Acts 13:16-17, and 2 Corinthians 6:14-7:1.
Answer the questions below.

1. Who sentenced Yeshua to die by crucifixion?

2. Where was Yeshua crucified?

3. Which three women stood at the foot of Yeshua's cross?

4. What was written on the sign above Yeshua's head?

5. What did the soldiers do with Yeshua's garments?

6. On what day was Yeshua crucified?

7. What type of branch did the soldiers use to give Yeshua sour wine?

8. With what did a soldier pierce Yeshua's side?

9. Who led the Israelites out of Egypt?

10. "For we are the ____ of the living God."

Bo WORD SEARCH

Read Exodus 10:1-13:16. Find and circle the words below.

FIRSTBORN

BLOOD

DARKNESS

PHARAOH

LINTEL

LAMB

MULTITUDE

JEWELRY

ISRAELITES

BITTER HERBS

UNLEAVENED BREAD

HYSSOP

All about Bo...

Draw a picture to retell the story of Yeshua's crucifixion.

Imagine you are an Egyptian. What would you say to the Israelites as they left Egypt?

....
....
....
....
....
....
....
....

This Torah Portion shows me...

....
....
....
....
....
....

What do you eat for the Passover meal? Draw your own Passover.

Bo

"Yah said to Moses, "Go in to Pharaoh, for I have hardened his heart and the heart of his servants, that I may show these My signs among them."

Exodus 10:1

Bo

"Go!"

בֹּא

Trace the Hebrew word here:

Write the Hebrew word here:

Let's discuss...

Open your Bibles and read the Bible verses below.
Discuss these questions with your family, friends, and classmates.

1. Read Exodus 10:1-11:10 and Romans 9:17.
Why do you think Yah hardened Pharaoh's heart?

2. Read Exodus 12:1-28.
How did the Israelites honor the first Passover in Egypt?

3. Read Exodus 12:17.
Yah asked His people to honor the Passover meal and Feast of Unleavened Bread forever. How do you honor these Appointed Times?

4. Read Exodus 12:1-13:16 and Leviticus 23.
The Spring Feasts (Appointed Times) were fulfilled by Yeshua 2000 years ago. Which is your favorite mo'edim? Why?

5. Read Exodus 12:1-13:16 and John 19:1-37.
How do the Passover and Feast of Unleavened Bread point to Yeshua?

Beshalach TORAH QUIZ

Read Exodus 13:17-17:16. Answer the questions below.

1. After leaving Goshen, towards which sea did the Israelites go?

2. Whose bones did the Israelites take with them?

3. How did Yah lead the Israelites through the wilderness?

4. Which army chased after the Israelites?

5. How did Yah separate the waters of the Red Sea?

6. How did Yah stop the Egyptians from following the Israelites?

7. To which wilderness did the Israelites go after crossing the sea?

8. How did Yah feed the Israelites?

9. How did Yah give the Israelites water at Rephidim?

10. Who led the Israelites into battle with the Amalekites?

Beshalach PROPHETS QUIZ

Read Judges 4:4-5:31. Answer the questions below.

1. Who was Deborah's husband?

2. What were Deborah's two roles?

3. Where did Deborah sit to give judgment?

4. Who did Deborah tell to lead the Israelites in a battle against the Canaanites?

5. Who was the king of Canaan?

6. What did Barak tell Deborah in Judges 4:8?

7. How many men went into battle against the Canaanites?

8. In which place did Barak attack the Canaanites?

9. In whose tent did Sisera hide?

10. How long did the land have rest in Judges 5:31?

Beshalach
APOSTLES QUIZ

Read Romans 9:15-23, 1 Corinthians 10:1-13, and Revelation 15:1-4. Answer the questions below.

1. What did Yah say to Moses?

2. Why did Yah raise up Pharaoh?

3. Who was the spiritual rock that followed the Israelites in 1 Cor 10:4?

4. What happened to the Israelites with whom Yah was not pleased?

5. "Do not be _____ as some of them were…"

6. How many Israelites died in a single day in the wilderness?

7. Who must we not test?

8. Yah is _____.

9. How many angels and plagues are seen in Heaven?

10. What type of sea is mentioned in Revelation 15:2?

Beshalach WORD SEARCH

Read Exodus 13:17-17:16. Find and circle the words below.

```
V W R C R B J B Q Z Q N H R E
M L U E S H J Q V P Z W P N G
D K H Q P C K F G I C A C S Y
G Q X X M H I K E B Z T H K P
S L N E Z X I I I U K E A L T
S T P Z N C L D S V Q R R H I
J A R K Y T B O I O S A I A A
R Q B O J D B P T M P K O H N
M V K B N C E I N P I W T O S
Q A I L A G B O D N L S S R C
M A N N A T W H Y R L X B S E
X Y W E S K H I S V A E P E U
Y H R W I C E W N N R L B S C
M O S E S W Y Y Y W D K H Z O X
Q A M A L E K I T E S F O P F
```

PILLAR

MANNA

STRONG WIND

AMALEKITES

REPHIDIM

CHARIOTS

SABBATH

HORSES

QAIL

EGYPTIANS

WATER

MOSES

All about Beshalach...

Draw a picture to retell the battle at Rephidim.

Imagine you are an Israelite. Describe what it was like to cross the Red Sea.

....
....
....
....
....
....
....
....
....

This Torah portion teaches me…

....
....
....
....
....
....

Design a chariot for Pharaoh. Use your imagination!

"At twilight you shall eat **meat**, and in the **morning** you shall be filled with **bread...**"

(Exodus 16:12)

Beshalach

"When Pharaoh had let the people go, Yah didn't lead them by the way of the land of the Philistines, although that was near; for Yah said, "Lest the people change their minds when they see war and return to Egypt…"
Exodus 13:17

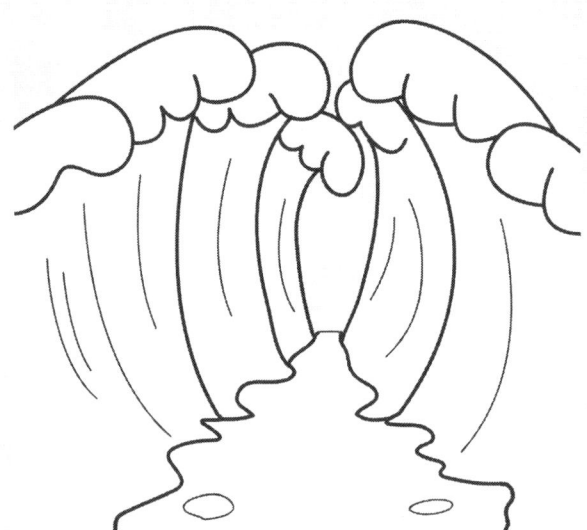

Beshalach

"When He let go"

בְּשַׁלַּח

Trace the Hebrew word here:

בשלח

בשלח

Write the Hebrew word here:

Let's discuss...

Open your Bibles and read the Bible verses below.
Discuss these questions with your family, friends, and classmates.

1 **Read Exodus 13:17-22.**
The Israelites left Egypt on the first day of Unleavened Bread. Who was leading them? Where did He lead them?

2 **Read Exodus 14:1-9.**
What did Pharaoh decide to do? How did Moses deal with the frightened Israelites?

3 **Read Exodus 15:1-19.**
How did the Israelites celebrate crossing the Red Sea?

4 **Read Exodus 12:8,15.**
Once the Israelites left Egypt, they had to "get the Egypt out of them." Yah instructed the Israelites to keep the leaven out of their houses during the Feast of Unleavened Bread. In our walk with Yeshua, what does this symbolize?

5 **Read Exodus 16.**
The Israelites were told to rest on the Sabbath and not gather manna. How do you honor the Sabbath?

6 In this Torah Portion, the Israelites went from praising Yah to defeatism and complaining. How does this compare to your walk with Yeshua when you face trials?

Yitro TORAH QUIZ

Read Exodus 18:1-20:26. Answer the questions below.

1. What relation was Jethro to Moses?
2. Who were Moses' two sons?
3. What did Moses do after he listened to Jethro's advice?
4. In what month did the Israelites arrive at Mount Sinai?
5. What did Yah do on the morning of the third day?
6. How did Yah answer Moses in Exodus 19:19?
7. On which mountain were the Israelites given the Ten Commandments?
8. Which day is holy and set-apart for Yah?
9. What will happen if you honor your mother and father?
10. What type of altar did Yah tell the people to build?

Yitro PROPHETS QUIZ

Read Isaiah 6:1-7:6 and 9:6-7. Answer the questions below.

1) Who died in the year Isaiah saw Yah sitting upon a throne?

2) What garment filled the temple?

3) How many wings did each seraphim have?

4) What did one of the seraphim have in his hand?

5) Who could not attack Jerusalem?

6) Who was in league with Ephraim?

7) Why did the heart of Ahaz and his people shake with fear?

8) Who did Yah instruct to go and meet Ahaz?

9) Who had devised evil against Judah?

10) His name shall be called Wonderful Counselor, Mighty God, Everlasting Father, _____ of Peace.

Yitro
APOSTLES QUIZ

**Read Matthew 19:16-30, 1 Timothy 3:1-13, and James 2:8-13.
Answer the questions below.**

1. What question did the man ask Yeshua in Matthew 19:16?

2. How did Yeshua answer the man in Matthew 19:17?

3. What else did Yeshua tell the man to do in Matthew 19:21?

4. Why did the man go away, full of sorrow?

5. Who will judge the twelve tribes of Israel?

6. Why must new believers not be put in leadership?

7. What type of character must leaders' wives have?

8. How do we fulfil the Torah?

9. How should we speak and act?

10. What triumphs over judgment?

Yitro Word Search

Read Exodus 18:1-20:26. Find and circle the words below.

```
P L X T H U N D E R L W K O T
E L E N Q Y L I H J C E P F E
O L F A D E L J U D G E S F N
P V I G D A N Y Z H J D Y E C
L T Q G E E O A I B E L R R O
E C V F H Z R Q C A T U X I M
O T J R J T A S M T H Q Q N M
F G S V U V E W H D R R Y G A
I W M H J U S N B I O K X S N
S I E Z O B L Y I V P O G M D
R Q I A J F E P M N K E Y O M
A M N T O J A H H U G W G S E
E V M L N N M R W W Z B T E N
L V M O U N T S I N A I M S T
L A N D O F M I D I A N Y W S
```

JUDGE
MOSES
MOUNT SINAI
LIGHTENING
TEN COMMANDMENTS
LEADERSHIP
PEOPLE OF ISRAEL
OFFERINGS
JETHRO
LAND OF MIDIAN
THUNDER
SHOFAR

All about Yitro...

How would you describe Jethro?

....
....
....
....
....
....
....
....

Imagine you were at Mt Sinai. Write a diary entry for the day Yah gave Israel His commandments.

....
....
....
....
....
....
....
....
....

This Torah portion teaches me…

....
....
....
....
....
....

Draw the Israelites' camp at Mount Sinai.

The ten commandments

Read Exodus 20.
Write the ten commandments on the tablets.

Yitro

"Jethro, the priest of Midian, Moses' father-in-law, heard of everything that Yah had done for Moses and for Israel His people; how Yah had brought Israel out of Egypt."

Exodus 18:1

Yitro

"Jethro"

יִתְרוֹ

Trace the Hebrew word here:

יִתְרוֹ

יִתְרוֹ

Write the Hebrew word here:

Let's discuss...

Open your Bibles and read the Bible verses below.
Discuss these questions with your family, friends, and classmates.

1. **Read Exodus 19:1.**
Which Appointed Time (mo'edim) occurs in the third month, 50 days after the Feast of Unleavened Bread? How do you honor this Feast?

2. **Read Exodus 18:13-27.**
Why do you think Jethro told Moses to appoint leaders over the people of Israel?

3. **Read Exodus 18:13-27, 1 Peter 5:3, and Mark 10:35-42.**
According to Yeshua, how should leaders behave? Do you see examples of this in your family or congregation? Discuss the role of a servant leader.

4. **Read Exodus 20 and Deuteronomy 5:2-5.**
Can you name the Ten Commandments? Who spoke these Words?

5. **Read Exodus 20.**
How do the first five commandments differ from the last set of five commandments?

6. **Read Exodus 20:8.**
Do you honor the Sabbath? If so, what do you do?

Mishpatim TORAH QUIZ

Read Exodus 21:1-24:18. Answer the questions below.

1. Hebrew slaves must work for how many years?

2. What is the punishment for murder in Exodus 21:12?

3. How much must a person repay for stealing or killing an ox or sheep?

4. Every seventh year, what should happen to the land?

5. What did Yah ask the Israelites to do on the seventh day?

6. What type of bread is eaten during the Feast of Unleavened Bread?

7. On which three Feasts should males appear before Yah?

8. Who should the Israelites not bow down to in Exodus 23:23-24?

9. What did the twelve pillars near the altar represent?

10. How long was Moses on Mount Sinai?

Mishpatim PROPHETS QUIZ

**Read Jeremiah 33:25-26 and 34:8-22.
Answer the questions below.**

1. Which king made a covenant with the people?

2. Who freed their Hebrew slaves?

3. "At the end of _____ years, you must set free your Hebrew slave who has served you six years."

4. What was the people's punishment for taking back their slaves?

5. With whom did Yah make a covenant?

6. From which land did Yah bring the Israelites out of slavery?

7. How did the Israelites profane Yah's name?

8. Which army will defeat the Israelites?

9. Who will Yah hand over to the Babylonians?

10. Yah will desolate the cities of which tribe of Israel?

Mishpatim
APOSTLES QUIZ

**Read James 3:2-12, Hebrews 12:25-29, and Matthew 5:38-42.
Answer the questions below.**

1. "For we all _____ in many ways…"

2. "The _____ is a fire, a world of unrighteousness."

3. Who can tame the tongue?

4. The tongue is full of what?

5. What comes from the same mouth in James 3:10?

6. "Let us be grateful for receiving a _____ that cannot be shaken…"

7. Let us offer to God acceptable worship, with _____ and awe…"

8. What type of fire is Yah?

9. "If anyone asks you to walk one mile, go with him _____ miles."

10. Who should we not refuse in Matthew 5:42?

Mishpatim WORD SEARCH

Read Exodus 21:1-24:18. Find and circle the words below.

```
S S U I C R S V C D D S X D U
Q E L R W A B H F R R F K O N
D H V A F R N E A O X E N M L
A D L E V J S A A V O H X A E
V X U O N E O J A I U Y W L A
E F I R W T S J C N S O M T V
T E G A E N H D B Y I I T A E
H D Y X J C E D N W I T Q R N
Y F Y C F M E I A E Q U E I E
B X J I J U V G G Y W N T S D
R C O V E N A N T H Z X P N B
I Q P H B L Z B H J B B E Z R
D Q X Z W P I C I B A O Y C E
E C D H S U K K O T G Y R O A
G F I R S T F R U I T S G D D
```

SHAVUOT

SLAVES

ALTAR

CANAANITES

SEVENTH DAY

FIRST FRUITS

SUKKOT

BRIDE

OXEN

COVENANT

NEIGHBOR

UNLEAVENED BREAD

All about Mishpatim...

Draw a picture to retell the story of Exodus 24:9-11.

I honor the Feast of Unleavened Bread by…

....
....
....
....
....
....
....
....

This Torah Portion teaches me…

....
....
....
....
....
....

Draw a map showing Mount Sinai and the Israelites' campsite.

The Promised Land

Open your Bibles and read Exodus 23.
Answer the questions. Color the picture.

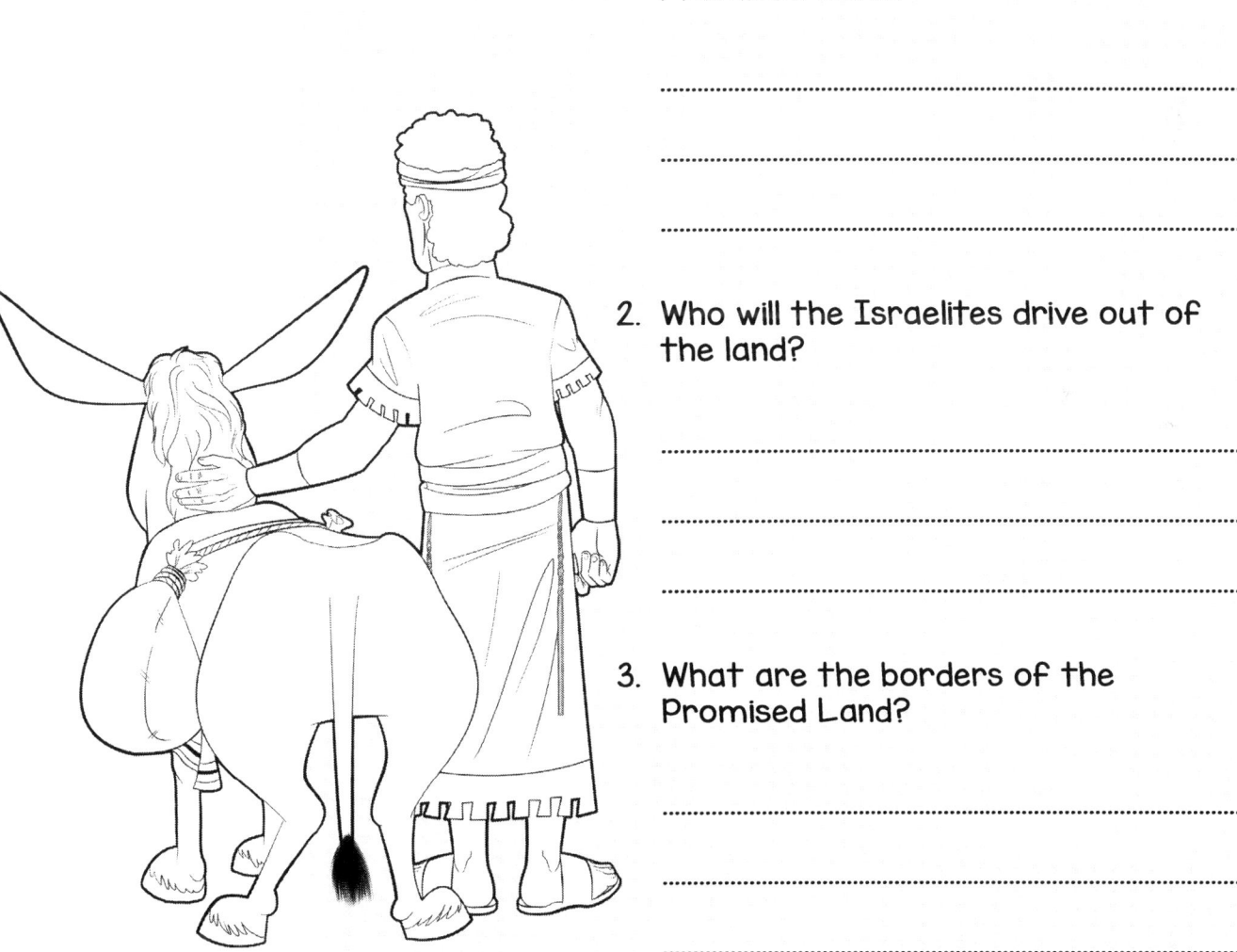

1. Who will lead the Israelites into the Promised Land?

   ....
   ....
   ....

2. Who will the Israelites drive out of the land?

   ....
   ....
   ....

3. What are the borders of the Promised Land?

   ....
   ....
   ....

Mishpatim

"Six days you shall do your work. On the seventh day you shall rest, that your ox and your donkey may have rest and the son of your servant and the alien may be refreshed."

Exodus 23:12

Mishpatim

"Laws"

מִשְׁפָּטִים

Trace the Hebrew word here:

מִשְׁפָּטִים

מִשְׁפָּטִים

Write the Hebrew word here:

Let's discuss...

Open your Bibles and read the Bible verses below.
Discuss these questions with your family, friends, and classmates.

1. Read Exodus 21-24.
What was the purpose of the Torah?

2. Read Exodus 23:1, James 3:2-12, and Proverbs 6:16,19.
Yah hates gossip. How can you stop yourself from gossiping about others?

3. Read Exodus 23:10-12.
Why is it important to honor the Sabbath? How do you honor this set-apart day?

4. Read Exodus 23:13.
The Torah clearly states to not worship false gods. How does this instruction apply to us today?

5. Read Exodus 23:10-19.
Why is it important to give to Yah? Why do you give to Yah? Do you notice any blessings in your life when you give generously?

6. Read Exodus 23:20, 1 Corinthians 10:4, and Acts 7:37-38.
Who was the angel who led the Israelites into the Promised Land?

Terumah TORAH QUIZ

Read Exodus 25:1-27:19. Answer the questions below.

1. What did Yah ask the Israelites to make?
2. What type of wood was used to make the Ark?
3. What did Yah say to place inside the Ark?
4. What metal did the Israelites use to make the mercy seat?
5. What was placed on each end of the Ark?
6. What food was to be regularly placed on the table?
7. How many branches does the lampstand (menorah) have?
8. What spiritual beings were included in the ten linen curtains?
9. What was placed on the four corners of the bronze altar?
10. What furnishings were placed inside the Most Holy Place?

Terumah PROPHETS QUIZ

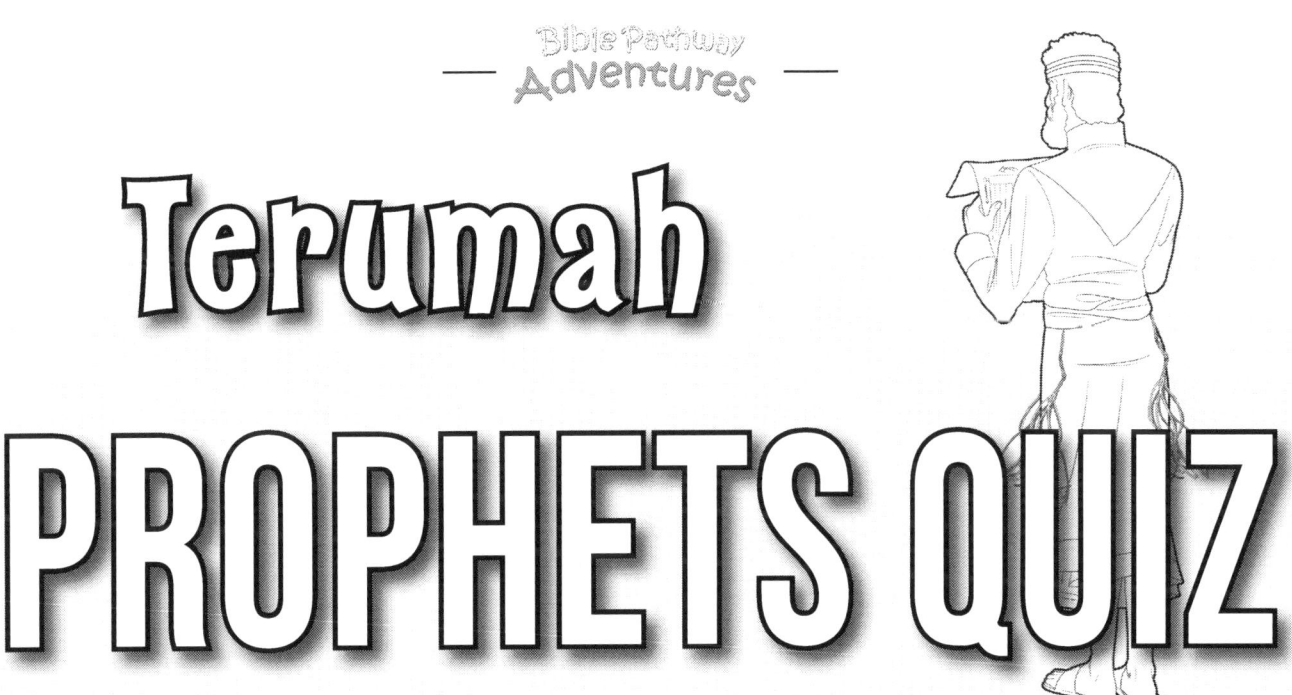

Read 1 Kings 5:26-6:13. Answer the questions below.

1. In what year of his reign did Solomon begin to build the temple (House)?

2. In which month did Solomon begin to build the temple?

3. How long ago did the Israelites leave Egypt?

4. Who was Solomon's father?

5. How long, wide, and high was the temple?

6. What type of window frames did Solomon use?

7. Why was the stone prepared at the quarry?

8. On what side of the temple was the entrance to the lowest story?

9. What type of wood did Solomon use to build the ceiling?

10. What did Yah promise Solomon and the Israelites if they followed His instructions?

Terumah APOSTLES QUIZ

Read Hebrews 10:19-22, 13:10-12, and Matthew 5:14-16.
Answer the questions below.

1. How do we have confidence to enter the holy place?

2. Who is our high priest today?

3. "Draw near with a true heart in full assurance of _____."

4. Where are the bodies of animals burned?

5. Where did Yeshua suffer?

6. Why did He suffer in this place?

7. "You are the _____ of the world."

8. "A city on a _____ cannot be hidden."

9. Where do people put their lamps?

10. Why should we let our light shine before others?

Terumah WORD SEARCH

Read Exodus 25:1-27:19. Find and circle the words below.

```
B R O N Z E A L T A R A K A H
R K S W N V E F C I Q K I C O
V Z H V Q J N N C F H Y T A L
I W M E N O R A H B Z N A C Y
K G W B P R B M V X Q F B I O
G O A T S K I N T W V B E A F
Q G V O U L C V E Z M B R W H
A D L U M Q T U P U W S N O O
V Y G Z O I F W R L I B A O L
M E R C Y S E A T T T L C D I
W K V A D Y W F U R A Y L C E
R S F Z Q D L S X U A I E W S
M C H E R U B I M E C R N U W
C O N T R I B U T I O N K S Z
J S H O W B R E A D B N Z E M
```

SHOWBREAD

BRONZE ALTAR

GOAT SKIN

CONTRIBUTION

CHERUBIM

MENORAH

ARK

MERCY SEAT

CURTAINS

ACACIA WOOD

TABERNACLE

HOLY OF HOLIES

All about Terumah...

Draw the Ark of the Covenant.

Describe how the Israelites got their gold, silver and bronze in Egypt.

....
....
....
....
....
....
....
....

This Torah portion teaches me…

....
....
....
....
....
....

Draw a picture of the Tabernacle in the wilderness.

Ark of the Covenant

Open your Bibles and read Exodus 25.
Answer the questions. Color the picture.

1. What type of wood was used to build the Ark?

   ....
   ....
   ....

2. How many golden cherubim were put on the Ark?

   ....
   ....
   ....

3. Where on the Ark did the Israelites put the mercy seat?

   ....
   ....
   ....

Terumah

"Yah spoke to Moses, saying, "Speak to the children of Israel that they take an offering for Me. From everyone whose heart makes him willing you shall take My offering. This is the offering that you shall take from them: gold, silver, bronze…"

Exodus 25:1-3

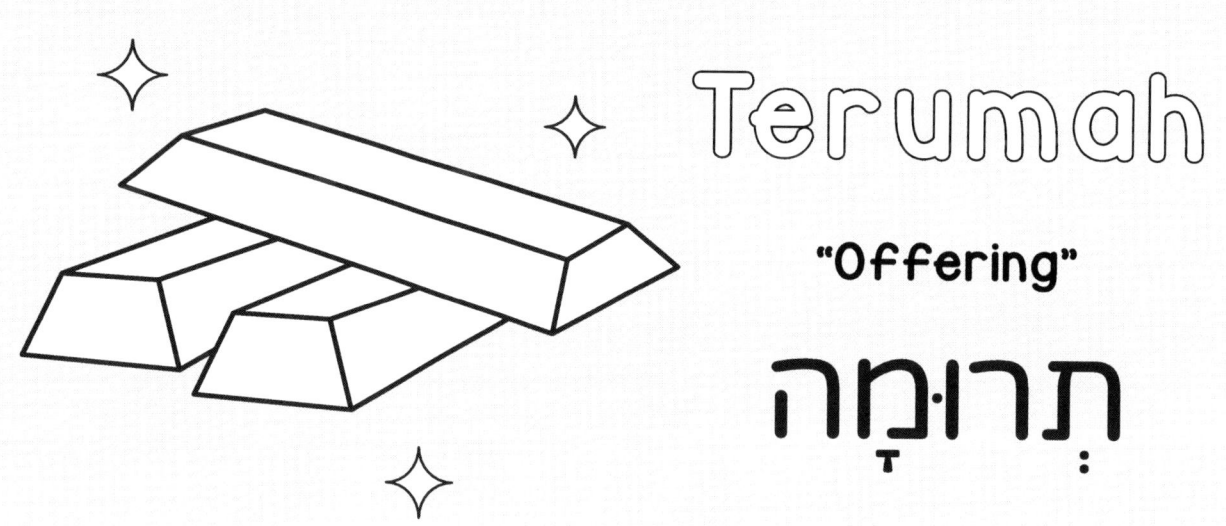

Terumah

"Offering"

תְּרוּמָה

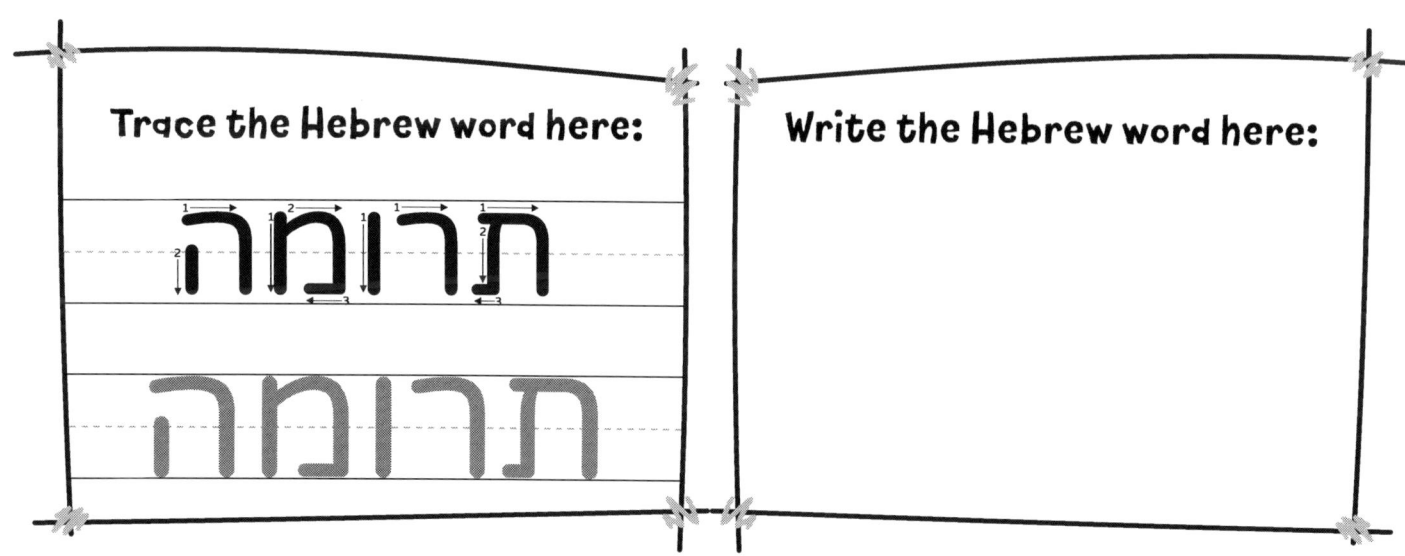

Trace the Hebrew word here:

Write the Hebrew word here:

Let's discuss...

Open your Bibles and read the Bible verses below.
Discuss these questions with your family, friends, and classmates.

1 Read Exodus 25:1-10.
Why did Yah want the Israelites to build a Tabernacle?

2 Read Exodus 25:1-2 and 2 Corinthians 9:7.
Yah likes us to give willingly and with the right attitude. How can you be generous with your family, friends, and neighbors? What should our heart attitude be when giving to the work of Elohim?

3 Read Exodus 25:31-40.
Do some research. What do the branches of the lampstand (menorah) represent?

4 Read Exodus 26:1-37.
What furnishings were placed in the Holy of Holies?

5 Read Exodus 26:1-37.
Research God's Appointed Times (mo'edim). On which Appointed Time did the high priest enter the Holy of Holies. How do you honor this Feast?

Tetzaveh TORAH QUIZ

Read Exodus 27:20-30:10. Answer the questions below.

1. What type of oil is used for the lamp?
2. Which three men did Yah choose to serve as priests?
3. What six garments did the High Priest wear?
4. What names were engraved on the onyx stones?
5. How many stones were placed on the breastplate of the High Priest?
6. What color was the robe of the ephod?
7. What animals were used to consecrate the priests?
8. What type of wood was used to make the altar?
9. What did Yah tell the Israelites to burn on the altar?
10. How often must Aaron make atonement on the horns of the altar?

Tetzaveh PROPHETS QUIZ

Read Ezekiel 43:10-27. Answer the questions below.

1. What did Yah tell Ezekiel to describe to the Israelites?

2. The whole territory on the top of the _____ shall be most holy.

3. How high is the altar?

4. What shape is the altar hearth?

5. Which direction do the steps of the altar face?

6. From which family are the Levitical priests?

7. For what type of offerings is the altar used?

8. Where is some of the bull's blood placed around the altar?

9. What three animals are used for burnt offerings?

10. "For _____ days you shall provide daily a male goat for a sin offering…"

Tetzaveh
APOSTLES QUIZ

**Read Hebrews 5:1-10, 13:10-17, and Romans 12:1.
Answer the questions below.**

1. How should we present ourselves to Yah?

2. How do high priests deal with the ignorant and wayward?

3. Which high priest was called by Yah?

4. Who appointed Yeshua as our high priest?

5. "You are a priest forever, after the order of _____."

6. Why did Yah hear Yeshua's prayers?

7. How did Yeshua learn obedience?

8. Who is the source of salvation to those who obey Him?

9. "Do not neglect to do good and _____ what you have…"

10. Why should we obey our leaders and submit to them?

Tetzaveh WORD SEARCH

Read Exodus 27:20-30:10. Find and circle the words below.

```
C T B R F G B R R C Z O S D I
Q O E R M X E B K G V R V H N
Z E E N E E B O F G M A O I C
H J P C T A X D B Y B L V G E
G O L D A O S I F B M T J H N
L T T F Y Q F T S V I A J P S
U I I Q D F U M P B V R S R E
D Q W W G T L A E L A T P I R
T I V T G P H S Z E A W A E E
F U Z S I D H U P Z T T D S G
U Q W T G W P I M L F I E T N
R A Z A I Z U M E M H W N O L
I P R I L U V Z A B I H U G I
M X K O L I V E O I L M A U E
A T O N E M E N T E P H O D O
```

ABIHU

HIGH PRIEST

GOLD

ATONEMENT

THUMMIM

ALTAR

INCENSE

OLIVE OIL

TENT OF MEETING

EPHOD

URIM

BREASTPLATE

All about Tetzaveh...

Draw the altar of incense.

Imagine you are a priest in the Tabernacle. Describe your job.

....
....
....
....
....
....
....
....

This Torah portion teaches me...

....
....
....
....
....
....

Draw the high priest in the Tabernacle.

Tetzaveh

"You shall command the children of Israel, that they bring you pure olive oil beaten for the light, to cause a lamp to burn continually. In the tent of meeting, outside the veil which is before the covenant, Aaron and his sons shall keep it in order from evening to morning before Yah…" *Exodus 27:20-21*

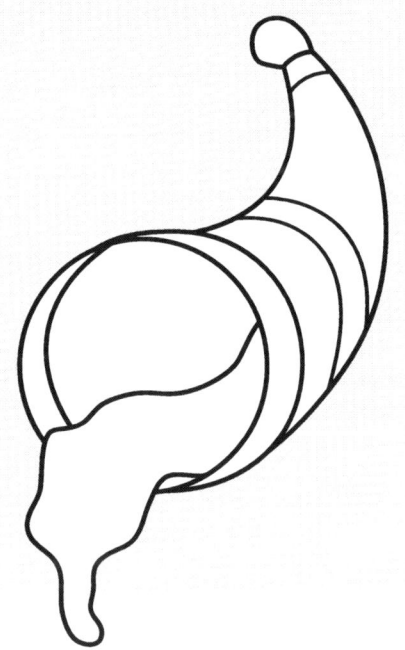

Tetzaveh

"You shall command"

תְּצַוֶּה

Trace the Hebrew word here:

Write the Hebrew word here:

Let's discuss...

Open your Bibles and read the Bible verses below.
Discuss these questions with your family, friends, and classmates.

1. Read Exodus 27:20-21 and Matthew 26:36-46.
Olive oil was used for anointing and burning in the menorah. Olives were pressed/crushed to produce oil for light. How does this process of making olive oil relate to our walk with Yeshua?

2. Read Exodus 28:15 and Revelation 21:12-14.
The high priest's breastplate contained twelve stones; one for each tribe of Israel. How does this relate to the twelve gates in the New Jerusalem?

3. Read Exodus 28.
Make a list of the garments worn by the priests. When did they wear these special clothes?

4. Read Exodus 28:29.
The priest wore the breastplate over his heart. How do you think Yeshua will judge us when we stand before Him?

5. Read Exodus 29:1-4 and Revelation 19:18.
In what condition does Yeshua expect His Bride when He returns? What does comparing these two bible passages teach us?

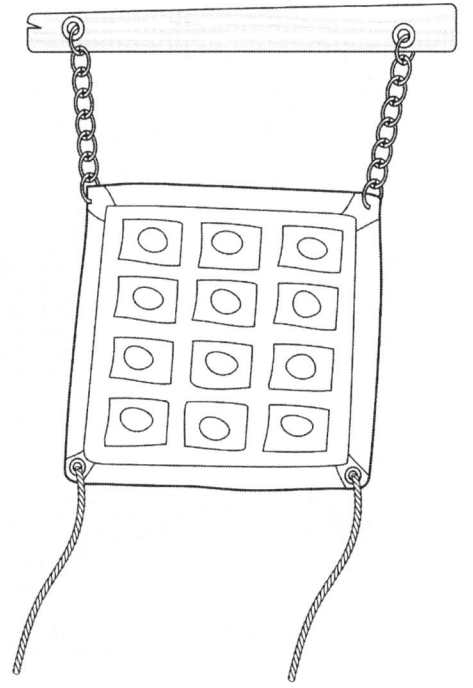

Ki Tisa TORAH QUIZ

Read Exodus 30:11-34:35. Answer the questions below.

1. How many shekels did Yah say to give as an offering?

2. Which metal was used to make the basin?

3. Which two men were chosen to make furnishings for the Tabernacle?

4. What Appointed Time is a sign between Yah and His people?

5. What animal did Aaron make out of gold?

6. Why did Moses throw the stone tablets on the ground?

7. How did Moses destroy the golden calf?

8. How did Moses punish the Israelites for worshiping a golden calf?

9. On which three mo'edim were Israelite men told to appear before Yah every year?

10. Which mountain did Moses climb with the two stone tablets?

Ki Tisa PROPHETS QUIZ

Read 1 Kings 18:1-39. Answer the questions below.

1. What instructions did Yah give Elijah?

2. Where was the famine severe?

3. Who cut off the prophets of the Lord?

4. How many prophets did Obadiah hide in caves?

5. What did Obadiah feed the prophets?

6. How many false prophets did Elijah summon?

7. On what mountain did Elijah meet the prophets?

8. Why did Elijah choose twelve stones to build an altar?

9. How many jars were used to pour water on the sacrifice and wood?

10. What did the people do when they saw the fire of Yah?

Ki Tisa APOSTLES QUIZ

Read 1 Corinthians 12:1-31, Acts 7:39-42, and Hebrews 3:1-6.
Answer the questions below.

1. Who is our high priest?

2. Who has been counted worthy of more glory than Moses?

3. "Moses was faithful in all God's house as a _____..."

4. Who is the builder of all things?

5. Who refused to obey Yah?

6. What instructions did the Israelites give Aaron?

7. What animal did Aaron make out of gold?

8. "There are varieties of gifts, but the same _____."

9. "For in one Spirit we were all _____ into one body…"

10. What has Yah appointed for the congregation of Israel?

Ki Tisa Word Search

Read Exodus 30:11-34:35. Find and circle the words below.

```
G M S A B B A T H M X K J O S
T X S P O R Y I Y O I S T H L
Y D E S T D D A G U Y P E O N
B R O N Z E R D Y N W N N L I
V T C G F D C P W T Q B S I G
P T A E O G M Z V S Y E R A O
N C L B N X O V U I N Z S B L
B R O L L S L W P N V A Z K D
A D X V O E U P R A W L V K E
R L M S E I T S U I U E I L N
A P Z K C N C S Q T A L M Z C
J H M J Y F A K F L R C Q C A
F Z E W N Q V N C R A F H P L
B Q H O L Y M D T B A S I N F
C M C O M M A N D M E N T S W
```

BEZALEL

TABLETS

HOLY

OHOLIAB

MOUNT SINAI

GOLDEN CALF

COMMANDMENTS

SABBATH

CENSUS

BRONZE

BASIN

COVENANT

All about Ki Tisa...

Draw Moses and the Ten Commandments.

Complete this sentence: After Moses came down from Mt Sinai, he…

....
....
....
....
....
....
....
....

This Torah portion teaches me…

....
....
....
....
....
....

Draw a set of pictures to retell the story of the golden calf.

"**They have made a golden calf and have worshiped and sacrificed to it...**"

(Exodus 32:8)

Ki Tisa

"Yah spoke to Moses, saying, "When you take a census of the children of Israel, according to those who are counted among them, then each man shall give a ransom for his soul to Yah when you count them, that there be no plague among them when you count them." *Exodus 30:11-12*

Ki Tisa

"When you take"

כִּי תִשָּׂא

Trace the Hebrew word here:

Write the Hebrew word here:

Let's discuss...

Open your Bibles and read the Bible verses below.
Discuss these questions with your family, friends, and classmates.

1. Read Exodus 30:17-21.
What was the bronze basin (laver) used for?

2. Read Exodus 30:17-38.
Yah required His priests to wash themselves and anoint themselves and all the furniture in the Tabernacle. What does this show us about how Yah likes things to be?

3. Read Exodus 31:1-11.
Oholiab and Bezalel were gifted artisans. What talents has the Father given you? How do you use these talents to serve Him and others around you?

4. Read Exodus 31:12-17.
How do you honor the Sabbath? What are the benefits of keeping this day set apart for Yahweh?

5. Read Exodus 32.
Why was Yah angry at the Israelites? How did Moses react to Yah's threat to destroy them for their idol worship?

6. Read Exodus 34:10-28.
Yah asked the Israelites to honor His Appointed Times (mo'edim) of Unleavened Bread, Shavuot, and Sukkot. How do you prepare and honor these Feasts?

Vayakhel TORAH QUIZ

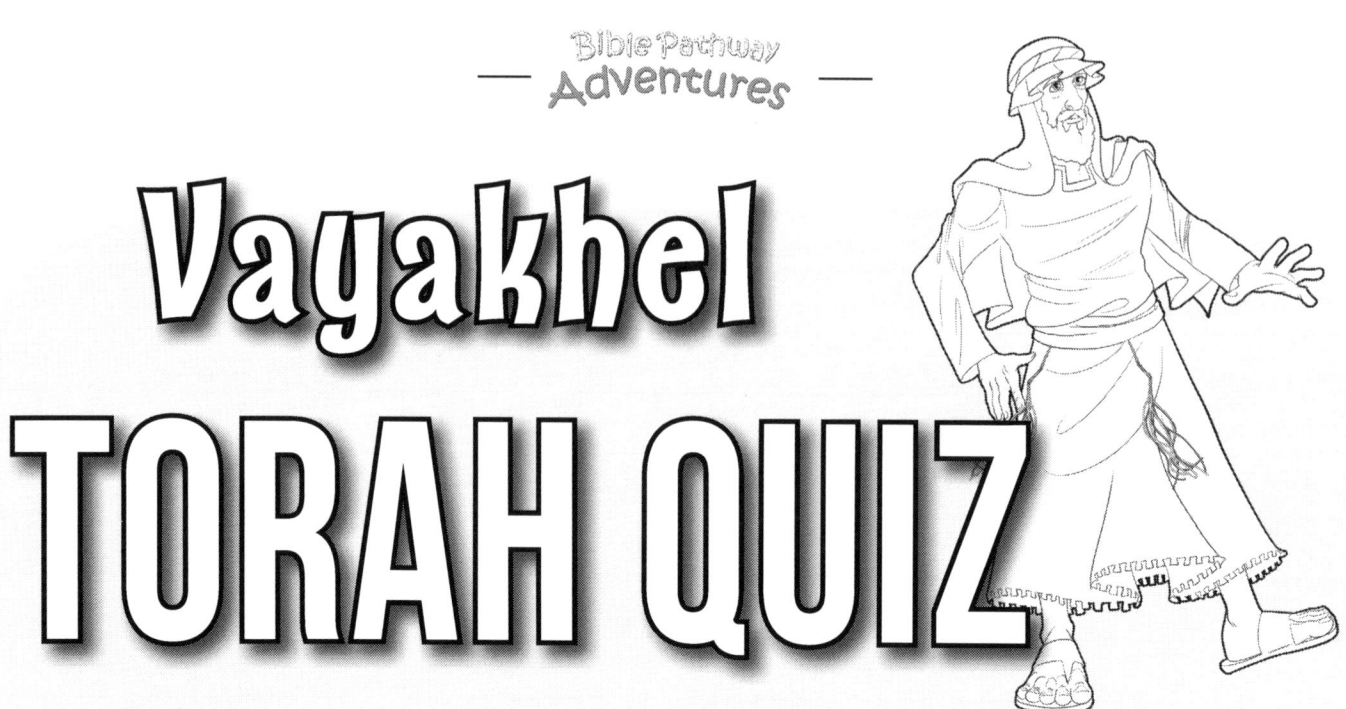

Read Exodus 35:1-38:20. Answer the questions below.

1. What did Yah tell the Israelites to do on the seventh day?

2. Why did Yah ask the Israelites for onyx and other precious stones?

3. What type of craftsman were chosen to make the Tabernacle and furnishings?

4. Oholiab was of which tribe of Israel?

5. How many curtains were made for the Tabernacle?

6. What wood was used to make the Ark of the Covenant?

7. What metal covered the Table of Showbread?

8. How many branches are on the lampstand (menorah)?

9. Where were the four horns placed on the altar?

10. What metal was used to make the tent pegs for the Tabernacle?

Vayakhel PROPHETS QUIZ

Read 1 Kings 7:13-26, 40-50. Answer the questions below.

1. Why did King Solomon send for Hiram?
2. Hiram was of which tribe of Israel?
3. How high were the temple pillars?
4. What type of bronze fruit was placed on the latticework?
5. Where were the pillars placed in the temple?
6. What were the names of the two pillars?
7. In what directions did the oxen face?
8. In which place did Hiram cast the vessels for the temple?
9. Why did Solomon not weigh the vessels for the temple?
10. How many lampstands (menorahs) were placed in the temple?

Vayakhel APOSTLES QUIZ

Read Hebrews 9:1-28, 2 Corinthians 9:1-15, and Hebrews 10:26-31. Answer the questions below.

1. What furnishings were placed inside the Holy Place?

2. What furnishings were placed into the Most Holy Place?

3. What was inside the Ark of the Covenant?

4. Who is the mediator of the renewed covenant?

5. In the wilderness, what did Moses sprinkle over the book, people and the tent of meeting?

6. "It is appointed for man to die once, and after that comes ____."

7. Why will Yeshua appear a second time?

8. What type of giver does Yah love?

9. "Whoever sows ____ will also reap bountifully."

10. What happens to people who set aside the law of Moses?

Vayakhel Word Search

Read Exodus 35:1-38:20. Find and circle the words below.

```
H F T Z R Q F I M C Y S P C X
A O S E D V H Q Q A C A P O L
I L L N N V W U D P R B S N M
S K M Y A T U L M B A B F G D
R N P O P O P V H U F A R R F
A E Y A N L A E I U T T M E B
E B Q X B D A R G I S H E G A
L S B W P R B C A S M I N A G
I B C I A J O R E C E B O T X
T B O A M Z A N A C N C R I M
E W D T H O S Z Z N X W A O O
S V I E Q G L Z F E C S H N S
I M Q O S B N S D Q W H O Y E
O G Y Y P R I E S T S E J F S
J H Y A L T A R O Q C Q W Q T
```

MENORAH
CRAFTSMEN
TENT PEGS
ALMOND BRANCH
CONGREGATION
ALTAR
HOLY PLACE
SABBATH
ISRAELITES
BRONZE
PRIESTS
MOSES

All about Vayakhel...

Draw the lampstand and table, altar of incense, and the bronze basin.

Yah loves a generous giver. Describe a time when you gave generously.

This Torah portion teaches me…

What's inside the Ark of the Covenant? Read Hebrews 9:4 and draw the items.

The Tabernacle

The Tabernacle was a sacred place where Yah met the Israelites during the forty years they lived in the desert. It represented His throne on the earth and symbolized His dwelling among His people. It was here the Israelites came together to worship Yah and offer sacrifices. The Tabernacle was a tent-like structure covered by animal skins surrounded by a white linen fence. The Tabernacle itself was divided into two places – the Holy Place and the Holy of Holies – and only the priests could enter these areas. All the furniture in the Holy Place was made of gold, just as Yah instructed.

It was the job of the Levites to carry the Tabernacle and set it up wherever the Israelites pitched camp. When the Levites erected the Tabernacle, they placed it in the center of the camp. Moses, Aaron, and the priests camped on the east side next to the entrance, and the other tribes of Israel were grouped into four camps around the Tabernacle's outer fence.

Read Exodus 26:1-31:18. Answer the questions below.

1. What was the purpose of the Tabernacle?
2. Which two men were put in charge of building the Tabernacle?
3. What oil was used to keep the lamps burning in the Tabernacle?
4. What was the purpose of the brazen altar?
5. Where was the mercy seat located?

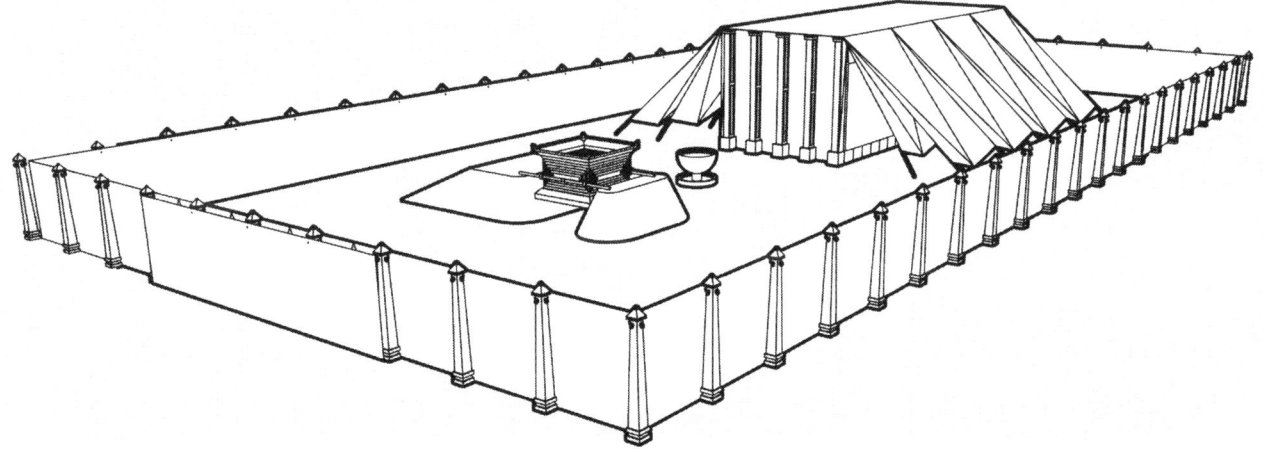

Vayakhel

"Moses assembled all the congregation of the children of Israel, and said to them, "These are the words which Yah has commanded, that you should do them."
Exodus 35:1

Vayakhel

"And he assembled"

וַיַּקְהֵל

Trace the Hebrew word here:	Write the Hebrew word here:
ויקהל	
ויקהל	

Let's discuss...

Open your Bibles and read the Bible verses below.
Discuss these questions with your family, friends, and classmates.

1 Read Exodus 35:1-3.
What were the Israelites instructed to do on the Sabbath? For how long did Yah expect His people to honor the Sabbath?

2 Read Exodus 35:4-29 and 2 Corinthians 9:6-15.
What does it mean to have a generous heart? Why do you think Yah loves a cheerful giver?

3 Read Exodus 35:30-35.
Bezalel and Oholiab were skilled craftsmen. What skills has the Father given you? How can you use these skills to bless others?

4 Read Exodus 35:30-36:7.
Many Israelites volunteered to help build the Tabernacle. How do you work with others to help people in your fellowship? Do you make yourself available?

5 Read Hebrews 9:1-5.
Why do you think Aaron's staff was placed inside the Ark of the Covenant?

Pekudei TORAH QUIZ

Read Exodus 38:21-40:38. Answer the questions below.

1. Who made all that Yah had commanded Moses?

2. How much gold was used to build the sanctuary?

3. How much bronze was used to build the Tabernacle?

4. What colored yarns were used to make the high priest's garments?

5. What was engraved on the onyx stones?

6. What stones were used for the high priest's breastplate?

7. What color was the high priest's robe?

8. On what day did the Israelites erect the Tabernacle?

9. Where did Moses put the altar of burnt offering?

10. What was on the Tabernacle by day and by night?

Pekudei Prophets Quiz

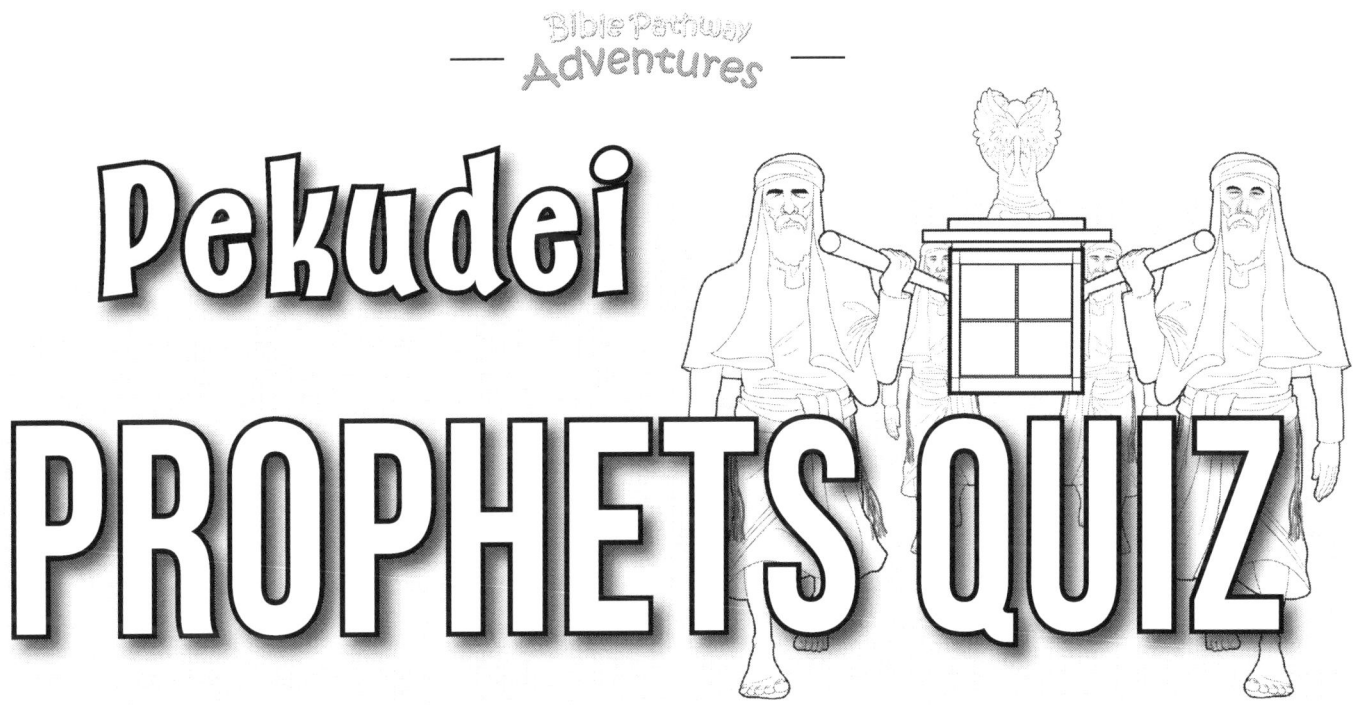

Read 1 Kings 7:51-8:21. Answer the questions below.

1. Who was Solomon's father?

2. Who did Solomon assemble in Jerusalem?

3. In which month did these men assemble in Jerusalem?

4. Where was the Ark of the Covenant kept before the temple was built?

5. How many sheep and oxen were sacrificed?

6. Where did the priests put the Ark of the Covenant?

7. What was inside the Ark of the Covenant?

8. In which place did Yah make a covenant with the Israelites?

9. Why could the priests not stand up?

10. Who was king of the Israelites at that time?

Pekudei
APOSTLES QUIZ

**Read Hebrews 5:1-11, 1 Corinthians 3:1-17, and Hebrews 7:1-8:6.
Answer the questions below.**

1. What does the high priest offer for sins?

2. Who appointed Yeshua as our high priest?

3. "You are a priest forever after the order of _____."

4. Which king met Abraham and blessed him?

5. How much of his spoils did the king of Salem give Abraham?

6. Which tribe of Israel serves as priests?

7. How were priests stopped from serving forever?

8. Who has been made perfect forever?

9. Who is the foundation of our faith?

10. "You are God's temple and God's _____ dwells in you…"

Pekudei Word Search

Read Exodus 38:21-40:38. Find and circle the words below.

```
Q S C I N A O V A O J Y T D X
B R E A S T P L A T E U W Z T
I L T A L E N T S T Q J E B U
E N G R A V E R J A T D L F M
A L Y F I A X C H B Y O V U U
W A J M I C R O I E O K E R M
D C S Q S I V K G R Y K T N W
U J C T R M U O H N W L R I K
V R N F L A Z G P A S Q I T M
V O D S Z S C A R C L H B U I
I C Q W V B T E I L E S E R O
S T F F I R E X E E Z L S E N
Z B U F M Z Z T S E D G A D Y
U V Z A M P W D T Q C E D M X
S H E K E L S K C L O U D F K
```

SHEKELS
ONYX
FURNITURE
HIGH PRIEST
ENGRAVER
TALENTS
FIRE
ARK
TABERNACLE
CLOUD
BREASTPLATE
TWELVE TRIBES

All about Pekudei...

Create a map of the Tabernacle for Moses.

How would you describe Bezalel's character?

....
....
....
....
....
....
....
....

This Torah portion teaches me…

....
....
....
....
....

Draw Aaron wearing the high priest's special clothes.

"**Yah** set apart the tribe of **Levi** to bear the ark of Yah's **covenant**..."

(Deuteronomy 10:8)

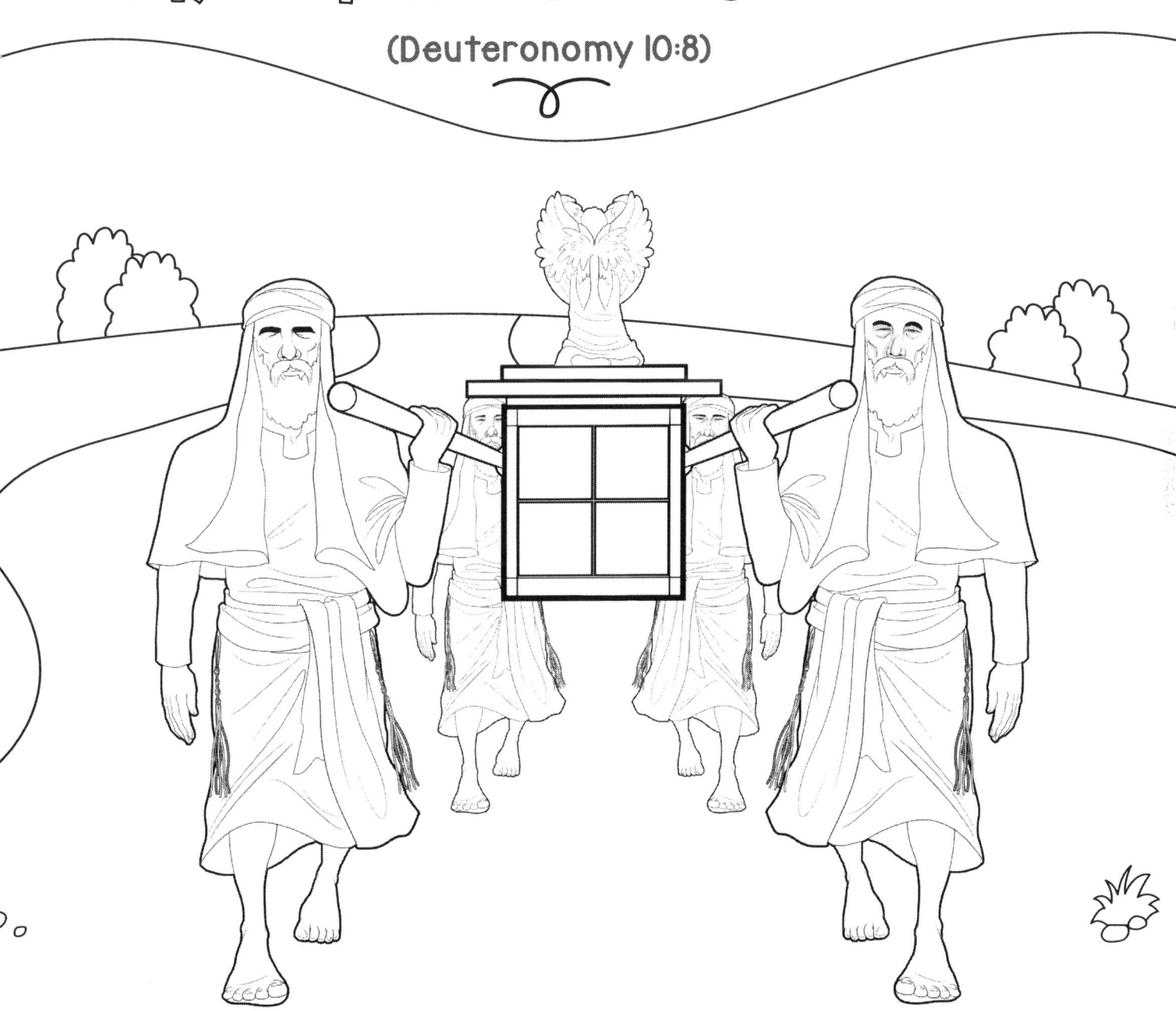

Pekudei

"These are the amounts of materials used for the Tabernacle, even the Tabernacle of the Testimony, as they were counted according to the commandment of Moses, for the service of the Levites by the hand of Ithamar, the son of Aaron the priest."

Exodus 38:21

Pekudei

"Amounts of"

פְקוּדֵי

Trace the Hebrew word here:

פְקוּדֵי

פְקוּדֵי

Write the Hebrew word here:

Let's discuss...

Open your Bibles and read the Bible verses below.
Discuss these questions with your family, friends, and classmates.

1. **Read Exodus 12:35-36, 35:5 and 21-24.**
   Where did the materials come from to build the Tabernacle?

2. **Read Exodus 40:36-38.**
   How did the Israelites know when to move and when to camp? How does the Father speak to us today?

3. **Read Exodus 39.**
   Name the high priests' garments. Who is our high priest today?

4. **Read Exodus 38:1-40:38.**
   Compare Moses to Yeshua. How many similarities can you come up with?

5. **Read Exodus 38-40 and 1 Corinthians 3:16-17.**
   The Israelites built the Tabernacle so Yah could dwell among them. Where is Yah's temple today?

ANSWER KEY

Shemot Torah quiz
1. He was afraid they would multiply and join the Egyptians' enemies
2. Kill the Hebrew baby boys and let the Hebrew baby girls live
3. Levi
4. Land of Midian
5. Zipporah, daughter of Jethro
6. Out of a burning bush
7. Go to Egypt, free the Israelites from slavery, and bring them out of Egypt
8. His hand became leprous like snow
9. His brother Aaron
10. He made the Israelites gather their own straw to make bricks, rather than his taskmasters giving them straw

Shemot Prophets quiz
1. World
2. Altar
3. Sun-pillars
4. Between the Euphrates River and the Vadi of Egypt
5. One by one
6. A great shofar will sound
7. On the holy mountain in Jerusalem
8. With stammering lips in a foreign accent
9. Precept by precept, line by line, a little here, a little there
10. Abraham

Shemot Apostles quiz
1. The God of Abraham, Isaac, and Jacob
2. Three months
3. Son of Pharaoh's daughter
4. Egypt
5. Beautiful
6. Moses was instructed in all the wisdom of the Egyptians
7. Forty years' old
8. In the wilderness of Mount Sinai
9. "I am the God of your fathers, the God of Abraham, Isaac, and Jacob."
10. The land of Egypt

Shemot word search puzzle

Worksheet: The Israelites are slaves
1. They would multiply and join the Egyptians' enemies
2. Made them work as slaves
3. Kill every Hebrew boy

Va'eira Torah quiz
1. Abraham, Isaac, and Jacob
2. Deliver them from slavery in Egypt and bring them into the land He promised to Abraham, Isaac, and Jacob.
3. Reuben
4. The staff turned into a serpent
5. Water turned to blood
6. Plague of gnats
7. Flies
8. The Egyptians' livestock
9. Hail
10. Land of Goshen

Va'eira Prophets quiz
1. From among the people/nations where they are scattered
2. All their neighbors
3. Pharaoh and all of Egypt
4. A great dragon
5. The river Nile
6. Forty years
7. Among the nations

8. Yah will gather the Egyptians from the peoples among whom they were scattered, restore the fortunes of Egypt, and bring them back to the land of Pathros and they shall be a lowly kingdom. It shall be the lowliest of the kingdoms and never again exalt itself above the nations.
9. In the twenty-seventh year, in the first month, on the first day of the month
10. King Nebuchadnezzar of Babylon

Va'eira Apostles quiz
1. "I will have mercy on whom I have mercy, and I will have compassion on whom I have compassion."
2. To show His power and so His name might be proclaimed in all the earth
3. The Israelites increased and multiplied in Egypt
4. Moses
5. Pharaoh's daughter
6. The land of Midian
7. After forty years
8. Because Moses was standing on holy ground
9. The land of Egypt
10. Yeshua Ha'Mashiach

Va'eira word search puzzle

Worksheet: Plague of frogs
1. Frogs came up and covered the land of Egypt
2. Egyptians' magicians
3. Pharaoh hardened his heart and would not free the Israelites

Bo Torah quiz
1. An east wind
2. Every green thing in the land of Egypt
3. Plague of darkness
4. So that Yah's wonders would be multiplied in the land of Egypt

5. Abih
6. Forever
7. Unleavened Bread (bread without yeast)
8. Death of the firstborn
9. Gold and silver jewelry, and clothing
10. About six hundred thousand men, plus women and children. A mixed multitude went with them, and flocks and herds of livestock

Bo Prophets quiz
1. A prophet
2. Nebuchadnezzar
3. The Pharaoh
4. The Egyptians
5. Memphis
6. Fatted calves
7. A beautiful heifer
8. The Babylonians
9. The children of Israel (the Israelites)
10. Jacob

Bo Apostles quiz
1. Pilate, the Roman governor
2. At Golgotha
3. His mother Mary, Mary (wife of Clopas), and Mary Magdalene
4. Yeshua of Nazareth, King of the Judeans
5. Divided them into four parts, one for each soldier
6. Preparation day for the Passover
7. Hyssop branch
8. A spear
9. Yah
10. Temple

Bo word search puzzle

Beshalach Torah quiz
1. Red Sea
2. Joseph's bones
3. A pillar of fire by night and a pillar of cloud by day
4. The Egyptian army
5. By a strong wind
6. He made sure their chariot wheels got stuck in the mud
7. Wilderness of Shur
8. He gave them quail and manna
9. He told Moses to strike the rock with his staff
10. Joshua

Beshalach Prophets quiz
1. Lappidoth
2. Prophetess and judge
3. Under a palm tree between Ramah and Bethel
4. Barak
5. Jabin
6. "If you go with me, I will go."
7. Ten thousand men (from the tribes of Naphtali and Zebulon)
8. Taanach
9. Heber
10. Forty years

Beshalach Apostles quiz
1. "I will have mercy on whom I have mercy, and I will have compassion on whom I have compassion."
2. To show His power and have His name proclaimed in all the earth
3. Yeshua
4. He overthrew them in the wilderness
5. Idolaters
6. 23,000
7. Yeshua
8. Faithful
9. Seven angels and seven plagues
10. Sea of glass mingled with fire

Beshalach word search puzzle

Yitro Torah quiz
1. Jethro was Moses' father-in-law
2. Gershom and Eliezer
3. Chose responsible Israelite men and made them leaders over the people (over thousands, hundreds, fifties and tens)
4. In the third month
5. Yah came down Mount Sinai
6. He thundered His reply to Moses
7. Mount Sinai
8. The Sabbath
9. Your days will be long in the land
10. An altar of earth to sacrifice burnt offerings and peace offerings

Yitro Prophets quiz
1. King Uzziah
2. The train of Yah's robe
3. Six wings
4. Burning coal
5. Rezin the king of Syria, and Pekah the son of Remaliah the king of Israel
6. Syria
7. Because the house of David had been told that Syria was in league with Ephraim
8. Isaiah and his son, Shear-jashub
9. Syria, with Ephraim and the son of Remaliah
10. Prince

Yitro Apostles quiz
1. What must I do to have eternal life?
2. If you want life, keep the commandments
3. Sell his possessions, give to the poor, and follow Me
4. He did not want to sell his possessions
5. Whoever has followed Yeshua
6. In case they become full of pride (puffed up with conceit)
7. Dignified, not gossips, sober-minded, and faithful in all things
8. Loving our neighbor as ourselves
9. As those who will be judged by the Torah (law of liberty)
10. Mercy

Yitro word search puzzle

Mishpatim word search puzzle

Mishpatim Torah quiz
1. Six years
2. Death
3. Five oxen for an ox and four sheep for a sheep
4. Let it rest and do not plant crops
5. Rest
6. Unleavened Bread
7. Unleavened Bread, Harvest (Pentecost), and Ingathering (Sukkot)
8. The false gods of the Amorites, Hittites, Perizzites, Canaanites, Hivites and the Jebusites
9. Twelve tribes of Israel
10. Forty days and forty nights

Mishpatim Prophets quiz
1. King Zedekiah
2. The people who had entered into the covenant
3. Seven
4. Their enemies will defeat them and take them into slavery
5. Israelites
6. Egypt
7. By taking back their male and female slaves
8. The army of the king of Babylon
9. King Zedekiah and his officials
10. Judah

Mishpatim Apostles quiz
1. Stumble
2. Tongue
3. No human being
4. Deadly poison
5. Cursing and blessing
6. Kingdom
7. Reverence
8. A consuming fire
9. Two
10. The one who would borrow from us

Worksheet: The Promised Land
1. An angel (Yeshua)
2. Hivites, the Canaanites, and the Hittites
3. From the Red Sea to the Sea of the Philistines, and from the wilderness to the Euphrates

Terumah Torah quiz
1. A sanctuary so that He could dwell in their midst
2. Acacia wood
3. The testimony (stone tablets with the commandments inscribed on them)
4. Gold
5. A golden cherubim
6. Bread
7. Six – three out of each side of the lampstand
8. Cherubim
9. Horns
10. Mercy seat and the Ark of the Covenant

Terumah Prophets quiz
1. Fourth year
2. Month of Ziv
3. 480 years
4. King David
5. Sixty cubits long, twenty cubits wide, and thirty cubits high.
6. Recessed frames
7. So no hammer or axe nor any tool of iron was heard in the house while it was being built
8. South side
9. Beams of cedar wood
10. Yah will establish His Word with Solomon, will dwell among the children of Israel, and not forsake them

Terumah Apostles quiz
1. Through the blood of Yeshua HaMashiach
2. Yeshua HaMashiach
3. Faith

4. Outside the camp
5. Outside the gate
6. In order to sanctify the people through His blood
7. Light
8. Hill
9. On a stand so it gives light to the whole house
10. So that people can see our good works and give glory to our Father

Terumah word search puzzle

Worksheet: Ark of the Covenant
1. Acacia wood
2. Two cherubim
3. On top of the Ark of the Covenant

Tetzaveh Torah quiz
1. Olive oil
2. Aaron, Nadab and Abihu
3. A breastpiece, an ephod, a robe, a coat of checker work, a turban, and a sash
4. The twelve tribes of Israel
5. Twelve stones
6. Blue
7. A bull and two rams
8. Acacia wood
9. Incense
10. Once a year

Tetzaveh Prophets quiz
1. The design of the temple
2. Mountain
3. One cubit high
4. Square
5. East

6. Zadok
7. Burnt offerings
8. On the four horns
9. Goat, ram, and bull
10. Seven

Tetzaveh Apostles quiz
1. As a living sacrifice
2. Gently
3. Aaron
4. His Father (Yah)
5. Melchizedek
6. Because of His reverence
7. Through what He suffered
8. Yeshua
9. Share
10. They keep watch over your souls, as those who will have to give an account

Tetzaveh word search puzzle

Ki Tisa Torah quiz
1. Half a shekel
2. Bronze
3. Bezalel and Oholiab
4. The Sabbath
5. A calf
6. He was angry the Israelites had made a golden calf
7. Melted it in the fire and ground it to dust
8. He forced them to drink gold dust
9. Feast of Unleavened Bread (including the Passover meal), Shavuot (Pentecost), and Sukkot (Tabernacles)
10. Mount Sinai

Ki Tisa Prophets quiz
1. Go and show yourself to Ahab, and I will bring rain upon the earth
2. In Samaria
3. Jezebel
4. One hundred
5. Bread and water
6. 850 prophets
7. Mount Carmel
8. One stone for each tribe of Israel
9. Four
10. Fell on their faces

Ki Tisa Apostles quiz
1. Yeshua
2. Yeshua
3. Servant
4. Yah
5. The ancient Israelites
6. "Make for us gods who will go before us. As for this Moses who led us out from the land of Egypt, we do not know what has become of him."
7. A golden calf
8. Spirit
9. Baptized
10. Apostles, prophets, teachers, miracles, then gifts of healing, helping, administrating, and various kinds of tongues (languages)

Ki Tisa word search puzzle

Vayakhel Torah quiz
1. Rest and set that day apart for Him
2. To make the ephod and breastpiece for the high priest
3. Skilled craftsmen
4. Dan
5. Ten curtains
6. Acacia wood
7. Gold
8. Six branches
9. One horn on each corner
10. Bronze

Vayakhel Prophets quiz
1. He was a skilled craftsman in bronze
2. Naphtali
3. Eighteen cubits' high
4. Pomegranates
5. At the vestibule of the temple
6. Jachin and Boaz
7. North, west, south, and east
8. Plain of the Jordan, between Succoth and Zarethan
9. Because there were so many of them
10. Ten menorahs (five on the south side and five on the north side)

Vayakhel Apostles quiz
1. Lampstand (menorah) and Table of Showbread
2. Altar of incense and Ark of the Covenant
3. Golden urn holding the manna, Aaron's staff, and the tablets of the covenant
4. Yeshua HaMashiach
5. Blood
6. Judgment
7. To collect those who are eagerly waiting for Him
8. A cheerful giver
9. Bountifully
10. They will die without mercy on the evidence of two or three witnesses

Vayakhel word search puzzle

Worksheet: The Tabernacle
1. For Yah to dwell among His people
2. Bezalel and Oholiab
3. Pure olive oil was used to light the lamps and keep them burning
4. The Israelites used the brazen altar to burn offerings and sacrifices
5. The mercy seat was on top of the Ark of the Covenant

Pekudei Torah quiz
1. Bezalel
2. Twenty-nine talents and 730 shekels
3. Seventy talents and 2,400 shekels
4. Gold, blue, scarlet and purple yarns
5. Names of the twelve tribes of Israel
6. Sardius, topaz, carbuncle, emerald, sapphire, diamond, jacinth, agate, amethyst, beryl, onyx, and a jasper
7. Blue
8. First day of the first month
9. At the entrance of the Tabernacle
10. The cloud of Yah was on the Tabernacle by day and fire in it by night

Pekudei Prophets quiz
1. David
2. The elders of Israel and all the heads of the tribes of Israel
3. Ethanim (seventh month)
4. City of David (Zion)
5. So many that they could not be counted
6. Inside the Most Holy Place (Holy of Holies)
7. Two stone tablets
8. Horeb
9. Because of the cloud (glory of Elohim) that filled the House
10. Solomon

Pekudei Apostles quiz
1. Gifts and sacrifices
2. The Father
3. Melchizedek
4. Melchizedek, king of Salem
5. A tenth
6. Levi
7. They died
8. Yeshua
9. Yeshua
10. Spirit

Pekudei word search puzzle

DISCOVER MORE ACTIVITY BOOKS!

Available for purchase at www.biblepathwayadventures.com

INSTANT DOWNLOAD!

- 100 Bible Quizzes
- 100 Bible Word Search
- Twelve Tribes of Israel
- Weekly Torah Portion
- Bereshit / Genesis
- Vayikra / Leviticus
- B'midbar / Numbers
- D'varim / Deuteronomy

Made in the USA
Las Vegas, NV
16 January 2023

65716383R00059